JN089232

A Healthy Life for Today and Tomorrow

The Society of English Studies

 Asahi Press

音声再生アプリ「リスニング・トレーナー」を使った 音声ダウンロード

朝日出版社開発のアプリ、「リスニング・トレーナー（リストレ）」を使えば、教科書の音声をスマホ、タブレットに簡単にダウンロードできます。どうぞご活用ください。

◉ アプリ【リスニング・トレーナー】の使い方

《アプリのダウンロード》

App Store または Google Play から「リスニング・トレーナー」のアプリ（無料）をダウンロード

App Storeはこちら▶ 　　Google Playはこちら▶

《アプリの使い方》

① アプリを開き「コンテンツを追加」をタップ
② 画面上部に【15670】を入力しDoneをタップ

音声ストリーミング配信 》》》

この教科書の音声は、右記ウェブサイトにて無料で配信しています。　　https://text.asahipress.com/free/english/

表紙デザイン：小林正明　　イラスト：ヨシオカユリ

はしがき

　一言で英語学習といっても、その目的に応じた目標設定、方法、動機付けなどは多岐にわたります。英語学習の目的が具体的であればあるほど学習意欲は高まるのではないでしょうか。本書は、『A Healthy Mind, A Healthy Body －今を生きるこころとからだ－』(2014)の後継書として作成されました。「健康とは何か」という根源的な問いに始まり、健康の身体的側面(インフルエンザ予防接種や睡眠が身体に及ぼす影響など)や心理的側面(動物に癒されることやAIの活用で精神面をサポートすることなど)を扱っている点については先行テキストを踏襲しています。英語を得意としない学生にも取り組み易いようイラストを多用しリーディングの文章を短めにしました。

　本書が先行テキストの精神を引き継いでいる点はレイアウトやデザインにも表れています。先行テキストでは、各ユニット1頁目のタイトル部分の番号の背景に薬草を想起させる葉が添えられています。本書では、葉はユニット内のセクション番号の背景として使われており、ユニット番号にはリンゴがあしらわれています。これは先行テキストのユニット1の最後にそえられている格言 An apple a day keeps the doctor away. がモチーフとなっています。

　世界的に猛威を振るう新型コロナウイルス感染症(COVID-19)を前に、わたしたちはつい神経質になってしまいます。対処法が明確でない脅威と対面した際には、致し方のない反応といえるでしょう。しかしこのような時だからこそ、ちょっとした遊び心やユーモアで心の余裕を保ちたいものです。本書の端々にはそのような思いが込められています。本書が提供するトピックを通じて学習者の皆さんが様々な事象について考え、英語力を向上させることを願っております。

2020 年
著者一同

本書の使い方

Section 1 Dialog

音声の会話文を聞いて質問の答えに適したイラストを選んでください。

必要な情報を汲み取るリスニングの練習が行えます。

Section 2 Words and phrases

本文（Section 3）で出てくる単語やイディオムを扱っています。

英語と日本語の意味を合わせて、本文の内容が理解し易くなるように、語彙を増やしていきましょう。

Unit 1 *What health means to us: maintaining our bodies and souls for today and tomorrow*

1 Dialog: Listen and answer the following questions.

Q1. What does Keiko think she uses too much?

a.   b.   c.

Q2. What is one way Shunji could change his lifestyle?

a.   b.   c.

Q3. What do both Shunji and Keiko like?

a.   b.   c.

2 Words and phrases

1) physical ( )	a. 身体の、肉体の
2) community ( )	b. 歯の、歯科の
3) infectious ( )	c. 宗教
4) aspect ( )	d. 健康な、健全な
5) dental ( )	e. 共同体、社会、集団
6) religion ( )	f. 伝染性の、伝染病の
7) sound ( )	g. 側面

1

---

3 Reading: What health means to us: maintaining our bodies and souls for today and tomorrow

What does "health" mean to us? Perhaps most people think about their physical health such as exercise, sleeping well, a flu shot, eating well, or staying fit. No one wants to be sick and suffer.

There are also other kinds of health, such as social health, mental
5 health, and spiritual health. Are community services available to everyone? Do we have good relationships with friends and neighbors? Do we feel sad for very long periods? What makes us feel complete and whole? Should we continue our normal lifestyles to keep the economy running while infectious diseases surround us? These are questions about social, mental, and spiritual
10 health.

No single kind of health makes us completely healthy. The combination and balance of various kinds of health are important. We should think about individuals and societies. In this textbook, we will learn about many aspects of health. This includes learning about the management of care-services, AI
15 and future technologies to improve medical treatments, and dental problems, to name a few. Health is also about daily activities such as what we eat, how natural hot springs can help us, how animals make us happy, and how important it is to have a good night's sleep.

A healthy community helps us maintain our mental and physical well-
20 being. Politics, the economy, culture, and, in some cases, religions, are all important for our bodies and souls to be safe and sound. All these come together to make us healthy.

Notes
infectious diseases 感染症   care-services 介護サービス

2

Section 3 Reading

各ユニットの中心部分となる本文です。音読や和訳などをしながら英文読解力の向上を目指します。

Section 4 Focus

本文の記事に関連した内容を正確に捉えられているか True or False の選択肢を選び理解度の確認をします。

Section 5 Comprehension quiz

本文の内容を確認する選択式問題です。内容にあったものを選んだり、文末を選び英文を完成させたりする出題形式があります。

4 Focus: T or F

1) Being healthy means only physical wellness. T / F
2) People are usually unhappy if their society is not managed well. T / F
3) AI might be only used to train medical students to be doctors. T / F
4) Politics and religions can also play important roles to keep a healthy society. T / F

5 Comprehension quiz

Q1. What's the main topic of this unit?
　　a. medical tests
　　b. exercise
　　c. food
　　d. health issues

Q2. How many types of health are introduced?
　　a. only one
　　b. two
　　c. four
　　d. none

Q3. In addition to individuals, what should we consider regarding health?
　　a. physics
　　b. finances
　　c. societies
　　d. responsibility

Q4. What examples are not mentioned?
　　a. AI
　　b. drug stores
　　c. hot springs
　　d. influenza vaccinations

6 Dialog: Listen to the dialog again and fill in the blanks.

Keiko: Shunji, do you think about your health?
Shunji: Yes, a lot, because my grandfather is not doing well.
Keiko: (1：　　). Have you checked community-based services?
Shunji: Yes. (2：　　). How about you, Keiko?
Keiko: I think I spend too much time using my smartphone.
Shunji: Maybe we should try (3：　　).
Keiko: Do you mean we should do more exercise? I'm not really into sports.
Shunji: (4：　　) taking walks or having a pet.
Keiko: I love animals. (5：　　) just by looking at them.
Shunji: I think they are good for our mental health, too.
Keiko: I agree. (6：　　).
Shunji: Right. We can make plans together.

　　a. I feel nice and happy　　　b. I was thinking more about
　　c. That must be hard for you　d. They are very helpful
　　e. We can do many things　　 f. to improve our lifestyle

7 Short writing

What aspect of health are you most interested in?

Section 6 Dialog

各ユニットのトピックの内容に合わせたサンプル会話です。Section1 のリスニングと同じ会話です。音読をしながら発音の練習や新たな会話表現を覚えましょう。

Section 7 Short writing

質問に対して、英語で答えましょう。間違いを恐れずに書いてみましょう。

CONTENTS

Unit 1 — What health means to us: maintaining our bodies and souls for today and tomorrow

1 Dialog: Listen and answer the following questions.

Q1. What does Keiko think she uses too much?

a.
b.
c.

Q2. What is one way Shunji could change his lifestyle?

a.
b.
c.

Q3. What do both Shunji and Keiko like?

a.
b.
c.

2 Words and phrases

1) physical ( )
2) community ( )
3) infectious ( )
4) aspect ( )
5) dental ( )
6) religion ( )
7) sound ( )

a. 身体の、肉体の
b. 歯の、歯科の
c. 宗教
d. 健康な、健全な
e. 共同体、社会、集団
f. 伝染性の、伝染病の
g. 側面

1

3 Reading: What health means to us: maintaining our bodies and souls for today and tomorrow

🔊 What does "health" mean to us? Perhaps most people think about their physical health such as exercise, sleeping well, a flu shot, eating well, or staying fit. No one wants to be sick and suffer.

There are also other kinds of health, such as social health, mental
5 health, and spiritual health. Are community services available to everyone? Do we have good relationships with friends and neighbors? Do we feel sad for very long periods? What makes us feel complete and whole? Should we continue our normal lifestyles to keep the economy running while infectious diseases* surround us? These are questions about social, mental, and
10 spiritual health.

🔊 No single kind of health makes us completely healthy. The combination and balance of various kinds of health are important. We should think about individuals and societies. In this textbook, we will learn about many aspects of health. This includes learning about the management of care-services*,
15 AI and future technologies to improve medical treatments, and dental problems, to name a few. Health is also about daily activities such as what we eat, how natural hot springs can help us, how animals make us happy, and how important it is to have a good night's sleep.

A healthy community helps us maintain our mental and physical well-
20 being. Politics, the economy, culture, and, in some cases, religions, are all important for our bodies and souls to be safe and sound. All these come together to make us healthy.

◀ **Notes** ▶ ··

infectious diseases 感染症　　**care-services** 介護サービス

4 Focus: T or F

1) Being healthy means only physical wellness.   T / F
2) People are usually unhappy if their society is not managed well.   T / F
3) AI might be only used to train medical students to be doctors.   T / F
4) Politics and religions can also play important roles to keep a healthy society.   T / F

5 Comprehension quiz

Q1. What's the main topic of this unit?

  a. medical tests

  b. exercise

  c. food

  d. health issues

Q2. How many types of health are introduced?

  a. only one

  b. two

  c. four

  d. none

Q3. In addition to individuals, what should we consider regarding health?

  a. physics

  b. finances

  c. societies

  d. responsibility

Q4. What examples are not mentioned?

  a. AI

  b. drug stores

  c. hot springs

  d. influenza vaccinations

6 Dialog: Listen to the dialog again and fill in the blanks.

Keiko: Shunji, do you think about your health?

Shunji: Yes, a lot, because my grandfather is not doing well.

Keiko: (1 :   ). Have you checked community-based services?

Shunji: Yes. (2 :   ). How about you, Keiko?

Keiko: I think I spend too much time using my smartphone.

Shunji: Maybe we should try (3 :   ).

Keiko: Do you mean we should do more exercise? I'm not really into sports.

Shunji: (4 :   ) taking walks or having a pet.

Keiko: I love animals. (5 :   ) just by looking at them.

Shunji: I think they are good for our mental health, too.

Keiko: I agree. (6 :   ).

Shunji: Right. We can make plans together.

a. I feel nice and happy	b. I was thinking more about
c. That must be hard for you	d. They are very helpful
e. We can do many things	f. to improve our lifestyle

7 Short writing

What aspect of health are you most interested in?

Unit 2 Chocolate may help you improve your health

1 Dialog: Listen and answer the following questions.

Q1. Which is the most natural way to take in polyphenols?

a. 　　b. 　　c.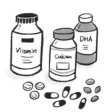

Q2. Which drink contains the most polyphenols?

a. 　　b. 　　c.

Q3. What do they plan to do on Saturday?

a. 　　b. 　　c.

2 Words and phrases

1) antioxidant agent	( )	a. を含む
2) cancer	( )	b. 精製（加工）食品
3) diabetes	( )	c. アレルギー
4) allergy	( )	d. 抗酸化剤
5) contain	( )	e. 飲食、食物、食生活
6) diet	( )	f. 癌
7) refined food	( )	g. 糖尿病

3 Reading: Chocolate may help you improve your health

(6) Do you want to eat more healthy food? But what in food is really good for our bodies? One good example may be polyphenols*. They are known as antioxidant agents and considered to be of help in slowing the development of diseases like cancer and diabetes. They are also believed to be good for
5 allergies, blood sugar levels, heart conditions, antiaging, stress reduction, and the damaging effects from smoking.

Chocolate is only one example of the many foods containing polyphenols. It is widely known that red wines are also said to be high in them. Other foods with polyphenols are fruits such as blueberries and
10 strawberries, vegetables like olives and spinach, nuts like walnuts and almonds, and some herbs such as dried oregano and dried rosemary, among many more. Drinks such as coffee, green tea, and black tea are also high in polyphenols, too.

(7) We should try to keep a well-balanced diet and eat various foods
15 regularly. It is said to be better to avoid deep fried foods and refined foods, which may destroy polyphenols. More than 8,000 types of polyphenols have been found and the most well-known are, perhaps, flavonoids*. A study shows that Japanese do not take in enough polyphenols in general. With correct information and ways of eating, we can hopefully stay healthy by
20 consuming polyphenols.

❘ Notes ❘▶ •

polyphenols ポリフェノール　　**flavonoids** フラボノイド

4 Focus: T or F

1) Polyphenols may be good for reducing stress.   T / F
2) Meat and processed food are high in polyphenols.   T / F
3) Polyphenol supplements help in growing fresh fruits like strawberries.

                                                                                                              T / F
4) There is no research about the effects of polyphenols at all.   T / F

5 Comprehension quiz

Q1. What may polyphenols not have an effect on?
   a. allergic reactions
   b. cuts and bleeding
   c. heart failure
   d. preventing cancer

Q2. What food may not be high in polyphenols?
   a. strawberries
   b. tea and coffee
   c. walnuts
   d. French fries

Q3. Which one should be avoided in order to take in polyphenols efficiently?
   a. chocolate
   b. deep fried chicken
   c. vegetables
   d. blueberries

Q4. Which is probably the best way to take in polyphenols?
   a. eating only chocolates and drinking lots of red wine
   b. eating processed food at every meal
   c. eating various kinds of food regularly
   d. taking as many polyphenol supplements as possible

Masa: Hello, Keiko. I studied a little about chocolate.

Keiko: Really? (1 :　　　).

Masa: Chocolate contains polyphenols. They are good for your health.

Keiko: (2 :　　　) chocolate is not only cacao and sugar?

Masa: That's right. But chocolate is not the only source. Another natural way to take in polyphenols is by eating fresh food like vegetables and fruits.

Keiko: (3 :　　　)

Masa: Yes, drinks like coffee and tea.

Keiko: That's great because I like them both. (4 :　　　)

Masa: Some nuts contain polyphenols, but it's best to have (5 :　　　), and take them regularly.

Keiko: (6 :　　　)

Masa: Little by little every day. We can make a list or food chart.

Keiko: Great. Let's do it on Saturday.

a. Do any drinks contain polyphenols?　　b. Do you mean

c. How about other food?　　d. How regularly, do you mean?

e. Tell me what you learned　　f. a well-balanced diet

7 Short writing

What would you say to encourage people to eat healthy food?

Unit 3 · Some people want to reduce the amount of time they spend on their phones

1 Dialog: Listen and answer the following questions.

Q1. How much time did she spend on her smartphone yesterday?

a.    b.    c.

Q2. What does she use her smartphone most for?

a.    b.    c.

Q3. What does she watch?

a.    b.    c.

2 Words and phrases

1) digital detox	( )	a. 再びつながる
2) wasting time	( )	b. 時間を浪費する
3) neglecting work	( )	c. 仕事を怠る
4) mood	( )	d. 〜と連絡を取る
5) cope without ...	( )	e. デジタル・デトックス
6) in contact with ...	( )	f. 気分、機嫌
7) reconnect	( )	g. 〜無しで済ます

3 Reading: Some people want to reduce the amount of time they spend on their phones

In the UK about one third of people went on a digital detox. What this means is that they decided to reduce the amount of time that they spend online and on their smartphones. But why did they do that? Most people were worried about wasting time, neglecting work, and not spending
5 enough time with friends and family. They said they want to improve their concentration, mood, and quality of sleep, as well as talk directly with their friends and family.

How do people reduce the time they spend on their smartphones? Some make a period of the day when they do not use smartphones, such as
10 mealtimes or times when commuting to work or school. Others decide not to take their phones into the bedroom, bathroom or toilet. When they are at home, some people decide to leave their smartphones in one place instead of carrying the phones around with them. This means that they do not check their phones all the time for emails and other messages. In some
15 cases, people delete apps on their phones, such as Twitter and Facebook.

A digital detox can be very stressful. Some people cannot cope without being able to shop online whenever they feel like it. Others miss not being able to play games online. For people who want to be in contact with their friends all the time, a digital detox can be very difficult. People who go on a
20 digital detox or who have finished one like reconnecting in person with people who are important to them.

4 Focus: T or F

1) Leaving your phone outside your bedroom means that you will use it less.

T / F

2) If you carry your phone around at home, you will probably check for messages very frequently. T / F

3) If you shop online a lot, a digital detox might be stressful. T / F

4) People on a digital detox miss talking directly with good friends. T / F

5 Comprehension quiz

Q1. What percentage of people in the UK last year tried to spend less time online?

a. 20

b. 33

c. 65

d. 95

Q2. What are people worried about?

a. not using time wisely

b. too much work

c. not enough friends

d. being too close to family

Q3. Where did some people decide not to take their phones?

a. work

b. train

c. kitchen

d. bedroom

Q4. What do people like about going on a digital detox?

a. shopping online   b. checking email

c. playing games   d. reconnecting in person with people

6 Dialog: Listen to the dialog again and fill in the blanks.

Sam: (1：)

Mai: Yes, I can check that by pressing this button. Yesterday, I spent six and a half hours on my phone.

Sam: (2：) What do you use your smartphone most for?

Mai: I spend a lot of time on SNS's.

Sam: (3：)

Mai: The rest of the time I spend watching videos.

Sam: (4：)

Mai: Most of all I like watching videos of animals.

Sam: Do you ever feel you spend too much time on your phone?

Mai: Yes, I do. (5：) And my friends complain that I ignore them.

Sam: Have you ever heard the expression "digital detox"?

Mai: Yes, but I'm not sure exactly what it means.

Sam: (6：)

a. Anything else?

b. Does your smartphone show your daily screen time?

c. I often feel bad about how much time I am wasting.

d. It means a period of time when people give up using smartphones.

e. That's quite a lot of time   f. What do you like watching?

7 Short writing

What is the best way to reduce the amount of time you use your smartphone?

1 Dialog: Listen and answer the following questions.

Q1. What kind of game is mentioned?

a. 　　b. 　　c.

Q2. What is the main topic of the conversation?

a. 　　b. 　　c.

Q3. What kind of medical operation is mentioned?

a. 　　b. 　　c.

2 Words and phrases

1) artificial　　(　　)
2) anxiety　　(　　)
3) judge　　(　　)
4) replacement　　(　　)
5) detection　　(　　)
6) diagnosis　　(　　)
7) come up with ...　　(　　)

a. ～を考案する
b. 発見
c. 交代
d. 人工の
e. 不安
f. 診断
g. を（批判的に）判断する

Artificial Intelligence (AI) is making a big impact on our lives in many ways. Let's look at three advantages of using AI technology to treat people with mental illnesses.

The biggest advantage is that AI robots might be able to replace human
5 doctors. Some patients don't like talking about their anxieties with doctors. With robots, however, patients can talk about their anxieties without worrying about being judged by real people. Also, this replacement can solve the shortage of doctors and nurses, too.

The second advantage is early detection of mental illness. Recently,
10 smartphone apps* supporting mental care have been developed. The app users have access to treatment that is less expensive than going to clinics. And some of these apps can be used for free. Once installed, they can use it any time they like.

The final advantage is better diagnoses and treatments. Some patients
15 may not like robots because they are impersonal*. However, robots with AI can help human doctors do a better job by giving them a lot of data about patients. Using the data, doctors can make better diagnoses and come up with better treatments.

Although there are some problems with AI, the use of robots with AI
20 has the potential to grow further and be more useful for human beings. Nevertheless, it is a new technology, so we need to be careful about how we develop and use it.

◀ **Notes** ▶ •

apps アプリ   **impersonal** 人間味のない

4 Focus: T or F

1) AI has a big influence on people's lives.   T / F

2) Smartphone apps can be useful for mental care.   T / F

3) There are no problems using AI for mental healthcare.   T / F

4) AI for mental healthcare should be abandoned quickly.   T / F

5 Comprehension quiz

Q1. Some patients don't like talking to doctors because (   ).

    a) doctors are friendly

    b) the patients don't trust doctors

    c) of personal judgements

    d) of early detection

Q2. What allows patients to get mental support any time they want?

    a) apps

    b) money

    c) data

    d) work

Q3. What is the third advantage of AI in mental healthcare?

    a) low cost

    b) inefficiency

    c) anxiety

    d) better diagnoses

Q4. Why do we need to be careful to develop and use AI?

    a) Because of the quality of video games

    b) Because of potential problems

    c) Because of hospitals' reputations

    d) Because of public transportation

6 Dialog: Listen to the dialog again and fill in the blanks.

Sam: I can't believe a computer program beat the chess champion.

Keiko: (1 :   ), isn't it?

Sam: It is, but I'm worried, because computers with AI are getting more and more advanced.

Keiko: (2 :   )?

Sam: AI might control us one day.

Keiko: (3 :   ). There are some (4 :   ) things about AI.

Sam: Like what?

Keiko: AI can provide medical services. AI robots that heal mental illness have been developed recently.

Sam: AI robots can heal human beings (5 :   ). How?

Keiko: Well, they can talk to patients and give (6 :   ) support.

Sam: That's great. My mother is having an eye operation tomorrow. I hope AI robots will be able to do it in the near future, too.

a. That's amazing   b. What's wrong with that

c. mentally   d. necessary

e. I don't think that will happen   f. positive

7 Short writing

How can we make better use of AI robots?

Japanese school lunches benefit children in many ways

🎧 **1** Dialog: Listen and answer the following questions.

Q1. What do the children ask their parents to do?

a.    b.    c.

Q2. What is one good point about school lunches?

a.    b.    c.

Q3. What can we learn from school lunches?

a.    b.    c.

2 Words and phrases

1) locally   (   )
2) struggle   (   )
3) affordable   (   )
4) decade   (   )
5) agri-food company   (   )
6) by contrast   (   )
7) nutritionist   (   )

a. （その）一方
b. 農業食品会社
c. 栄養士
d. 地元で、地域で
e. 苦戦する、もがく
f. 10年間
g. 手頃な（価格の）

3 Reading: Japanese school lunches benefit children in many ways

(15)   To Japanese people, school lunches mean balanced meals that are good for their health. The food used in school lunches is grown locally and almost never frozen first and reheated before being served.

    The principal at an elementary school in Tokyo said, "Parents hear their
5 kids talking about what they had for lunch. They even ask their parents to recreate the meals at home."

    Japanese people take both food and health seriously and school lunches are a point of national pride. While the Japanese school system has struggled in the past with school lunches, it was finally able to solve the puzzle by
10 creating school meals that are healthy, tasty, and affordable. This is the result of using a system that education officials describe as basically based on common sense.

(16)   In the United States, where obesity rates have tripled over the past three decades, a new school food service started creating menus that feature food
15 with fewer calories. But even the healthiest choices are generally foods provided by large agri-food companies, cooked off-site, frozen, and then reheated. And children prefer something fried, salty or sweet.

    Schools in Japan, by contrast, give children the sort of food that they would eat at home, not at stadiums or amusement parks. The meals are
20 often made from scratch. They're not only balanced but also tasty — with rice, vegetables, fish, and soups.

    When it comes to food in Japan, children are taught to eat what they are served, rather than leave the food on their plates. Most schools employ nutritionists who work with children who are picky or unhealthy eaters.

4 Focus: T or F

1) Locally grown food is usually frozen first before being served at schools in Japan.   T / F

2) Japan's school lunch system is something that the country can be proud of.

                                                                    T / F

3) Schools in Japan often buy food from stadiums.   T / F

4) Japanese school children normally go home to have lunch.   T / F

5 Comprehension quiz

Q1. In Japan, school lunches (   ).

    a. harm your health   b. are frozen food

    c. are cooked by parents   d. are balanced meals

Q2. Japanese school lunches (   ).

    a. were like a puzzle

    b. have beautiful designs

    c. are not so expensive

    d. are using officials

Q3. In the United States, (   ).

    a. the number of people who are overweight has increased in 30 years

    b. large agri-food companies do not offer meals at schools

    c. food is generally cooked by the school staff

    d. fried, salty, and sweet things are the healthiest choices in cafeterias

Q4. Japanese children (   ).

    a. have economic advantages

    b. revolt against their parents

    c. learn to eat whatever is on their plates

    d. are often unhealthy eaters

◯14 6 Dialog: Listen to the dialog again and fill in the blanks.

Kyoko: My children (1 :   ) cook lunch from a school-lunch recipe yesterday.

Harumi: My children also want to eat the (2 :   ) food as their school lunches, at home.

Kyoko: Really? (3 :   ).

Harumi: I guess (4 :   ) the food is not just healthy but also tasty.

Kyoko: We can (5 :   ) from school lunches.

Harumi: Yes, how to choose food that's good for your body, how to use fresh food in season, and how to develop good manners when you eat in public.

Kyoko: In the news, it says that Japan's school lunches are something like a model for (6 :   ).

Harumi: I hope it stays that way.

    a. I wonder why   b. asked me to

    c. it's because   d. learn a lot

    e. same kind of   f. the rest of the world

7 Short writing

In your experience, what were the good points of eating school lunches?

Unit 6 — Foods that contain hidden sugar and how to avoid them

1 Dialog: Listen and answer the following questions.

Q1. Where did Mai buy lunch?

a.

b.

c.

Q2. What is Sam having for lunch?

a.

b.

c.

Q3. How many grams of sugar are there in 245 grams of low-fat yoghurt?

a.

b.

c.

2 Words and phrases

1) add （　　　）
2) processed foods （　　　）
3) category （　　　）
4) contain （　　　）
5) avoid （　　　）
6) tin［can］（　　　）
7) label （　　　）

a. を含む
b. を避ける
c. ラベル、食品表示
d. 加工食品
e. を加える
f. カテゴリ、部門
g. 缶詰

3 Reading: Foods that contain hidden sugar and how to avoid them

(18) Hidden sugar is extra sugar that is added to processed foods to improve their taste. Let's look at foods that contain hidden sugar. One category is things that look healthy and seem to give us more energy. For example, low-fat yoghurt, granola bars, and sports drinks. People think that these foods
5 are healthy, but actually they are full of sugar. People do not know this. Other examples of food containing lots of hidden sugar are sauces, soups and salad dressings. These foods don't look sweet at all. Most people think they contain no sugar. Pre-made pasta and pizza sauces contain not only tomatoes but also a lot of added sugar. It is easy to forget about this.
10 Processed foods such as convenience-store foods or ready-made meals also contain a lot of sugar.

(19) Are you worried about hidden sugar? Here are two things that you can do right away to reduce the amount of sugar you eat. First, avoid pre-cooked meals that are sold in convenience stores. It is better to make food at home
15 because you know what is in it. Some people buy pasta sauce in a bottle or packet because it is quick and easy. How about making your own at home? All you need is a tin of tomatoes, a little butter, and some herbs, and you can make sugar-free pasta sauce in no time at all. Another thing you can do is to read the labels on the food you buy. Nowadays, most products list the
20 contents, and you can see the amount of sugar. If the sugar content is high, you can choose not to buy the product.

4 Focus: T or F

1) People generally know how much sugar is in a sports drink.　　T / F
2) The problem with bottled salad dressings is that they contain too much fruit juice.　　T / F
3) It is easy and quick to make healthy pasta sauce at home.　　T / F
4) Labels have no information about the amount of sugar.　　T / F

5 Comprehension quiz

Q1. Many people think that granola bars are (　　).

    a. low fat

    b. low in sugar

    c. healthy

    d. unhealthy

Q2. Pasta sauce sold in shops contains (　　).

    a. only tomatoes

    b. no sugar

    c. coloring

    d. added sugar

Q3. You can avoid added sugar by (　　).

    a. eating ready-made meals

    b. cooking at home

    c. buying convenience-store food

    d. eating at a restaurant

Q4. If you want to know how much sugar is in food, you should (　　).

    a. read the label

    b. buy a book

    c. ask the makers

    d. taste the food

6 Dialog: Listen to the dialog again and fill in the blanks.

Sam: The next class doesn't start until 1:00. Mai, did you (1 :   )

Mai: Yes, I just went to a convenience store.

Sam: What did you get?

Mai: I got a cappuccino and a low-fat yoghurt. Do you have anything for lunch, Sam?

Sam: Yes, I have a rice ball and a salad. (2 :   )

Mai: Yes, that would be nice. There are some free seats over there.

Sam: Did you know that low-fat yoghurt is not very healthy?

Mai: (3 :   ) It only contains yoghurt. It is low-fat and healthy. I eat it a lot.

Sam: Low-fat products (4 :   )

Mai: What does added sugar mean?

Sam: Makers add sugar (5 :   ) For example, 245 grams of low-fat yoghurt contains 47 grams of sugar. That is the same as 12 teaspoons of sugar.

Mai: Are you kidding? I thought it was so healthy.

Sam: That's what most people think. Added sugar is also in lots of other food. People (6 :   ) That is why it is called hidden sugar.

a. buy anything for lunch yet?   b. don't know that.

c. have a lot of added sugar.   d. Shall we eat together?

e. so that the product tastes better.   f. What do you mean?

7 Short writing

What is the best way to cut down on the amount of sugar you eat?

Unit 7 Periodontal disease can cause many other illnesses

1 Dialog: Listen and answer the following questions.

Q1. What is a sign of gum disease?

a.
b.
c.

Q2. How many people in their 20s in Japan have gum disease?

a.
about a half

b.
about two-thirds

c.
almost all

Q3. What is a cause of gum disease?

a.
b.
c.

2 Words and phrases

1) sticky   (   )
2) plaque   (   )
3) high blood pressure   (   )
4) blood vessel   (   )
5) suffer from ...   (   )
6) lung   (   )
7) effective   (   )

a. 高血圧
b. 効果的な
c. 〜に苦しむ
d. 粘着性の
e. 歯垢
f. 血管
g. 肺

3 Reading: Periodontal disease can cause many other illnesses

(21)   About 80% of Japanese adults have periodontal disease. It begins when the sticky, bacteria-filled film called plaque builds up around the teeth. After plaque builds up it will cause inflammation* of the gums, and finally you will lose your teeth if you don't take care of them. For many years, periodontal

5 disease has been said to be a cause of other diseases such as diabetes*, heart disease, and aspiration pneumonia*.

   Both periodontal disease and diabetes are called 'chronic diseases' and they can never be cured. Severe periodontal disease makes a lot of TNF-α* and it enters the blood and then prevents insulin from working properly.

10 That might lead to high blood pressure and then diabetes.

(22)   Severe periodontal disease may also cause heart disease. Periodontal-disease bacteria enter the blood vessels of the gums, combine with platelets*, and attach to the blood-vessel walls of the heart. They narrow or block vessels and cause heart disorders such as heart attacks.

15   In addition, aspiration pneumonia is said to be caused by periodontal-disease bacteria. Although pneumonia is a common illness even in healthy individuals, over 90% of people who are in their 80's or 90's with pneumonia suffer from aspiration pneumonia. Periodontal-disease bacteria were found in their lungs.

20   If you want to keep your teeth and your whole body healthy, you should brush your teeth often. Tooth brushing is the easiest and the most effective way to stop plaque from building up around the teeth.

◀ **Notes** ▶ ●

inflammation 炎症   **diabetes** 糖尿病   **aspiration pneumonia** 誤嚥性肺炎
TNF-α [Tumor necrosis factor alpha] 炎症性物質の一種   **platelet** 血小板

4 Focus: T or F

1) Only young Japanese people have periodontal disease.　　　T / F
2) You only lose your teeth because of plaque.　　　T / F
3) TNF-α can enter the blood, which may lead to some diseases.　　T / F
4) Brushing your teeth is the simplest way to prevent many diseases.　T / F

5 Comprehension quiz

Q1. In which country do about 80% of adults have periodontal disease?

a. USA

b. South Africa

c. Japan

d. Australia

Q2. What will you get when insulin does not work properly in your body?

a. periodontal disease

b. heart disease

c. aspiration pneumonia

d. diabetes

Q3. Which of the following is caused by periodontal-disease bacteria?

a. COVID-19

b. influenza

c. cancer

d. heart attacks

Q4. Which group of people are most likely to have aspiration pneumonia?

a. elderly people

b. young people

c. children

d. babies

6 Dialog: Listen to the dialog again and fill in the blanks.

Etsuko: Ah, my gums are bleeding a little.

Kenji: (1： 　)

Etsuko: No, but this may be the beginning of gum disease.

Kenji: (2： 　)

Etsuko: I've heard that about 70 percent of people in their twenties have gum disease in Japan.

Kenji: Wow! (3： 　)

Etsuko: Most people don't think of bleeding gums as a symptom.

Kenji: That's terrible! What causes it?

Etsuko: (4： 　) There are a lot of bacteria in plaque and they make your gums swell.

Kenji: Anything else?

Etsuko: (5： 　) Gum disease can cause other illnesses, too.

Kenji: If so, it is very important (6： 　), isn't it?

    a. But, you are still in your twenties!

    b. Do they hurt?

    c. to brush our teeth every day

    d. I didn't know that so many young people have that!

    e. It is mainly caused by plaque.

    f. Smoking and stress are also causes of gum disease.

7 Short writing

What is the best way to prevent periodontal diseases and diabetes?

Unit 8 *A regular lifestyle for a creative life*

 1 Dialog: Listen and answer the following questions

Q1. What do some great people do?

a. 　　b. 　　c.

Q2. Which is NOT included in the daily routines of famous people?

a. 　　b. 　　c.

Q3. Which of these people is mentioned as an example of a famous person?

a. 　　b. 　　c.

2 Words and phrases

1) routine	(　)	a.	～を最大限に活用する
2) frequently	(　)	b.	試行錯誤
3) punctual	(　)	c.	習慣的に繰り返されること
4) diligent	(　)	d.	体力
5) strength	(　)	e.	頻繁に
6) trial and error	(　)	f.	時間厳守の
7) make the most of ...	(　)	g.	勤勉な

3 Reading: A regular lifestyle for a creative life

(24) Is your lifestyle regular? Have you ever thought about improving your daily routine? Whether you have or not, you might get some ideas from the lives of famous people.

Famous people often have similar routines. Many, for example, get up
5 early, drink coffee or tea, and take walks frequently. In particular, early risers tend to focus on their work in the morning. Many also have three meals a day, making either lunch or dinner the main one. On the other hand, a few famous people are heavy smokers, or do too much exercise. There are also a few people who get up late and work in the late evening or at night or eat
10 only two meals or even just one meal a day. The interesting fact for all of them is that almost all seem to keep a daily routine in doing their creative work. A couple of people say that they are not so punctual or diligent and that they need a routine.

(25) A very famous Japanese novelist once decided to change his unhealthy
15 lifestyle completely. He gave up smoking, drank less alcohol, and made his meals center around vegetables and fish. He also started running every day. He says that he needs strength to write novels.

Daily routines depend on the person. So why don't you try to find the best routine for yourself? Famous people have created routines through trial
20 and error to make the most of their talent.

4 Focus: T or F

1) Some common habits can be seen among famous people.　　　　T / F

2) Unhealthy life habits never contribute to a creative life.　　　　T / F

3) One novelist dramatically changed his lifestyle.　　　　T / F

4) If you try to find a better lifestyle, you might find one that suits you.

　　　　T / F

5 Comprehension quiz

Q1. Which seems to be very important for becoming a creative person?

　　a. to keep to a regular routine

　　b. to eat a light meal three times a day

　　c. to have a lot of relaxing time

　　d. to do what other people don't do

Q2. What type of person did the Japanese novelist become?

　　a. a strict vegetarian

　　b. a person who eats meat a lot

　　c. a health-conscious person

　　d. a heavy drinker

Q3. What seems to be most important thing in leading a creative life?

　　a. to find daily routines that suit you

　　b. to keep early hours

　　c. to decide the times of eating meals in a day

　　d. to make a schedule

Q4. Which is the main idea of the passage?

　　a. Introducing only healthy daily routines

　　b. Explaining about unhealthy daily routines

　　c. Copying great people's unhealthy habits

　　d. Finding a good daily routine

6 Dialogue: Listen to the dialog again and fill in the blanks.

Minoru:	Naoko, are you interested in famous people's lifestyles?
Naoko:	(1 :)
Minoru:	I think we can learn something from them.
Naoko:	So, what are you going to learn from their lifestyles?
Minoru:	We can learn (2 :) For instance, what time they got up and went to bed, what food and drink they had.
Naoko:	(3 :) What sort of routine?
Minoru:	OK. Beethoven got up at sunrise and made coffee with great care.
Naoko:	Hmm. Do you (4 :)
Minoru:	Glen Gould. He's a pianist I really like. Do you know him?
Naoko:	(5 :)
Minoru:	He worked during the night hours and had only one meal a day!
Naoko:	Unlike Beethoven's. (6 :)
Minoru:	Michael Jackson was influenced by the Japanese diet and ate brown rice.

a. about their daily habits.　　b. Not much. Why?

c. Only by name.　　d. What about more recent people?

e. have another example?　　f. I'm getting the picture.

7 Short writing

How do you keep your brain sharp?

Unit 9 Pets can bring many good things into our lives

 1 Dialog: Listen and answer the following questions.

Q1. What are the two people talking about?

a.  b.  c.

Q2. How many pets are there at the time of this conversation?

a.  b.  c.

Q3. Why will Laura cry?

a.  b.  c.

2 Words and phrases

1) social skills	(	)	a.	～と交流する、～と触れ合う
2) interact with ...	(	)	b.	～から恩恵を受ける
3) look into ...	(	)	c.	落着き、平穏
4) benefit from ...	(	)	d.	社会的能力
5) calmness	(	)	e.	効き目がある
6) nursing home	(	)	f.	～を研究調査する
7) working	(	)	g.	高齢者福祉施設

3 Reading: Pets can bring many good things into our lives

(27) Having a pet can bring many good things into your life. The unconditional love of a pet will always give you a good feeling, when your pet is keeping you company. Pets can also decrease stress, improve heart health, and help children with their emotional and social skills.

5 Interacting with animals has been shown to decrease levels of cortisol* (a stress-related hormone) and lower blood pressure. Many studies have found that animals can reduce loneliness, increase feelings of social support, and improve your mood. Other researchers are looking into how animals might affect child development.

(28) 10 There are many other ways a pet can be of help. You might benefit from owning a dog to increase physical activity. You can walk your dog several times a day. Or, if your goal is to reduce stress, then watching a fish swim, for example, can give you a feeling of calmness.

Animals can serve as a source of comfort and support. Therapy dogs are 15 especially good at this. They're sometimes brought into hospitals or nursing homes to help reduce patients' stress and anxiety.

Pets also bring new responsibilities. Knowing how to care for and feed an animal is part of owning a pet. It's important for kids to be able to recognize signs of stress in their pets and know when not to approach them.

20 Researchers are trying to find out what's working, what's not working, and what's safe — for both the humans and the animals.

❙ **Notes** ❙▷ •

cortisol コルチゾール

4 Focus: T or F

1) There are different ways of interacting with animals depending on the goal of each person.   T / F

2) People staying at a hospital are never anxious or have stress.   T / F

3) Children can learn responsibility from taking care of animals.   T / F

4) Researchers are trying to find work for both the humans and the animals.   T / F

5 Comprehension quiz

Q1. What is <u>not</u> a benefit of owning a pet? It (   ).

     a. can keep a promise

     b. can be a friend to its owner

     c. could improve your health

     d. helps young owners develop social skills

Q2. Studies have found that animals can (   ).

     a. be a cause of stress   b. decrease a hormone related to stress

     c. increase blood pressure   d. feel social support

Q3. How can you increase physical activity with the help of a pet?

     a. Study hard and feel social support.

     b. Meet a therapy dog at a hospital.

     c. Watch a fish and get relaxed.

     d. Go outside with your dog and walk a couple of times a day.

Q4. Where do therapy animals serve as a source of comfort for patients?

     a. at school

     b. at the local drugstore

     c. at medical and welfare institutions

     d. in the park or on the beach

Sam: Hi, I heard you're (1 :   ) new homes for three puppies.

Jane: As a matter of fact, yes.

Sam: You know, when you have a pet, it's (2 :   ) being with a friend.

Jane: I know (3 :   ).

Sam: My daughter Laura would be so happy to have a puppy.

Jane: Let me show you their picture. (4 :   ) to decide.

Sam: Thank you! I'll tell her to be responsible and to (5 :   ) our new family member.

Jane: I think (6 :   ) to let children take care of pets.

Sam: I fully agree.

Jane: After a while, they can play outside together. Walking a dog can be great exercise, too.

Sam: I can't wait to see her cry for joy. See you!

Jane: Goodbye.

a. it's a good idea   b. just like

c. look after   d. looking for

e. Take your time   f. what you mean

7 Short writing

What kind of pet would you like to have? Why?

Community-based integrated care

1 Dialog: Listen and answer the following questions.

Q1. Which one could be the leading character in the movie Kenji saw?

a.

b.

c.

Q2. What does Kenji want to be?

a.

b.

c.

Q3. Which of the following shows you have completed a seminar on dementia?

a.

b.

c.

2 Words and phrases

1) dementia   (   )
2) frail   (   )
3) aging society   (   )
4) integrated care   (   )
5) older adults   (   )
6) promote   (   )
7) contribute   (   )

a. を推進する、を進める
b. 貢献する
c. 包括ケア
d. 高齢化社会
e. 高齢者
f. 虚弱、フレイル
g. 認知症

3 Reading: Community-based integrated care

Do you worry about getting dementia in the future? One in three Japanese people over 65 will have dementia by 2025. We cannot avoid aging and getting frail. We have become an "aging society."

The idea of community-based integrated care was introduced by the 5 government in 2013 to support older adults. The goal was to create a community to promote the health, safety, and peace of mind of those in need of care. It should be possible for people to walk to some type of community service within 30 minutes of their homes. Many community services also should be available to people.

10 One example is Team Eigenji in Shiga Prefecture that provides more complete care than the "integrated care" system. Medical professionals as well as others like police officers, local government officials, and volunteers take part in this. One doctor believes that no matter what a person's job is, they can all contribute.

15 Another example is a care facility in Kanagawa Prefecture. What is unique about it is that the residents and staff — even neighbors — come and spend time there as if it were their own home. One good example of this facility is when the older adult residents with dementia arranged a wedding ceremony for one of the staff members. The Japanese movie *Care-nin* is 20 based on that and the experiences of the president of this care facility in Kanagawa Prefecture. He says, "caring is only natural for everyone, so everybody can do it in their daily lives."

4 Focus: T or F

1) Community-based integrated care is a government policy.   T / F

2) Nonmedical professionals can join community-based integrated care.

    T / F

3) A care facility in Kanagawa Prefecture welcomes locals to spend some time with older adults there.   T / F

4) Caregivers and people with dementia are clearly divided in the facility.

    T / F

5 Comprehension quiz

Q1. What percentage of older adults over 65 may have dementia by 2025?

    a. 1.3%   b. 13%

    c. 33%   d. 65%

Q2. Why was community-based integrated care introduced?

    a. to criticize neighbors

    b. to save money

    c. to raise children

    d. to support those who are in need of care

Q3. What professions are mentioned as members of team Eigenji?

    a. police officers   b. athletes

    c. musicians   d. librarians

Q4. Which sentence is mentioned in the reading passage?

    a. Delivering meals to the local people

    b. People spending time at care facilities as if they were at their own homes

    c. Watching the older adults not doing anything

    d. Taking older adults to end-of-the-year parties

29 **6** Dialog: Listen to the dialog again and fill in the blanks.

Kenji: I saw a movie this weekend.

Mari: Oh, great, Kenji. (1 :　　)

Kenji: It's about a young man who works as a care worker.

Mari: (2 :　　) care-taking professions?

Kenji: Yes, I am. I got this orange wristband the other day.

Mari: (3 :　　).

Kenji: This is a kind of certificate of taking a short seminar on dementia.

Mari: So I guess (4 :　　) for people living with Alzheimer's disease.

Kenji: That's right. I'd like to work as a care provider in the future.

Mari: Oh, so you like (5 :　　).

Kenji: I liked the words to one of the songs in the movie, too.

Mari: Oh, what were the words?

Kenji: "At the beginning I thought I supported them, but finally I found myself (6 :　　)"

Mari: Yes, they are good words, aren't they?

a. Are you interested in   b. I might have seen it somewhere

c. looking after the elderly   d. What was it about?

e. being supported by them   f. the color orange represents support

7 Short writing

What would you say to encourage friends to care for people who have dementia?

40

Knotworking: beyond professionalism

 1 Dialog: Listen and answer the following questions.

Q1. What is Etsuko's job?

a.    b.    c.

Q2. Where does Etsuko think she can find good relationships?

a.    b.    c.

Q3. What does Etsuko plan to have next week?

a.    b.    c.

2 Words and phrases

1) professional   (   )
2) a national registered license   (   )
3) boundary   (   )
4) knot   (   )
5) facility   (   )
6) lecture   (   )
7) cooperate with ...   (   )

a. 〜と協力する、助け合う
b. 専門家
c. 国家資格
d. 施設
e. 結び目
f. 講義、講演、セミナー
g. 境界線

3 Reading: Knotworking: beyond professionalism

For healthcare workers, "professional" means that they must have a national registered license. They can take special care of patients, but many healthcare workers want to do more than that.

Many hospitals believe that they are caregivers and that patients are care receivers. However, healthcare workers at the Seichokai Medical Group in Osaka have started to call their patients "partners". They do this to break down the boundaries between them and their patients. How they treat their patients is important. It shows the value they add to local communities.

Another idea is "knotworking". This has been proposed by Yrjö Engeström, a Finnish professor. The word "knot" originally means a fastened piece of rope. It refers to key people or gathering places in a community. Knotworking is being used at Utsunomiya Hospital in Wakayama. A new facility called "Naru-comi" has been used not only for healthcare lectures but also for festivals of all kinds. People cooperate with each other as "knots". In this way, healthcare workers and patients became close community members. They finally found a way to help patients to continue active, healthy lives. They work hand in hand as "knots" to enable the community members to live happily together.

Although they take great pride in caring for patients at their workplaces, some local citizens do not appreciate the value and efforts of healthcare professionals. In the coming era of community-based integrated care, hospitals and other healthcare organizations need to work closely together and be good neighbors in local communities.

4 Focus: T or F

1) Every healthcare worker must have a national license.　　　T / F

2) Knot means to untie shoelaces in the Finnish language.　　　T / F

3) People achieve better results when they work in groups.　　　T / F

4) Many caregivers are proud of their jobs.　　　T / F

5 Comprehension quiz

Q1. What is a professional?

　　a. a person having a friend

　　b. a person living in a town

　　c. a person having a national registered license

　　d. a person studying in a school abroad

Q2. Who is Engeström?

　　a. a doctor at Utsunomiya Hospital

　　b. a volunteer at "Naru-comi"

　　c. a worker at the Seichokai Medical Group

　　d. a Finnish professor

Q3. What kind of service does "Naru-comi" provide?

　　a. medical care

　　b. transportation system

　　c. meetings and lectures

　　d. public health care

Q4. Why do professionals want to go beyond professionalism?

　　a. to support patients

　　b. to have more leisure time

　　c. to learn medical treatment

　　d. to be good neighbors

6 Dialog: Listen to the dialog again and fill in the blanks.

Keita: Etsuko, why did you decide to work in our hospital?

Estuko: Because I want to work at (1:) here.

Keita: Really? But you are a professional nurse, aren't you?

Estuko: Yes, but I want to do more to (2:) and make a place where we can work together. A farm is a great place to build good relationships.

Keita: Where did you get that idea from?

Estuko: I read (3:) knotworking.

Keita: I've heard about it. Does it (4:)?

Estuko: No. The word was first used by a Finnish professor called Engeström.

Keita: If we use knotworking, (5:) between healthcare workers and patients?

Estuko: Yes, I think so. I plan to have a barbecue party in front of our hospital next week. I (6:) healthcare workers, patients, and neighbors.

Keita: I think it's a great idea.

a. a book about   b. am going to invite

c. can we make a good relationship   d. have a Japanese origin

e. support the community   f. the organic vegetable farm

7 Short writing

Think of one way of creating a knotworking opportunity for your community.

44

Unit 12 *The health benefits of onsen*

 1 Dialog: Listen and answer the following questions.

Q1. Who are the speakers?

a.  b.  c.

Q2. Why are the speakers very tired?

a.  b.  c.

Q3. What will Mai do next?

a.  b.  c.

2 Words or phrases

1) benefit	( )	a. 不適切な
2) joint	( )	b. ～と人付き合いをする
3) effect	( )	c. 利益、恩恵
4) cure	( )	d. を治す、を癒す
5) soak	( )	e. 効果、影響
6) socialize with ...	( )	f. 浸す、つかる
7) inappropriate	( )	g. 関節

3 Reading: The health benefits of *onsen*

🔊36 In Japan, many people love going to public baths. There are two kinds of public baths. One is called an *onsen* and the other a *sentō*. A big difference is that hot natural spring water is used at *onsen*, while water from the public water-system is used at *sentō*.

5 *Onsen* are popular because of their physical-health benefits. They keep people warm and help their blood circulation. This is good for muscles and joints. Minerals in natural water have positive effects on our body. For example, chloride* helps to cure sore muscles*. Some minerals make your skin smooth and keep skin troubles away.

🔊37 10 *Onsen* are also good for your mental health. Soaking in a warm bath makes you feel relaxed and comfortable. The dressing rooms, bathing areas, and bathtubs at *onsen* are usually bigger than the ones at homes. Also, many *onsen* have open-air baths, sometimes with a great view of natural scenery. Spending time in such facilities refreshes your mind.

15 Talking with other people in the bath is a good way of enjoying *onsen* for social health. They have long been places where people not only take baths but also socialize with other people, having short conversations and sharing information. In some communities, *onsen* are known for supporting communication between people and building relationships.

20 There are also some issues, such as tattoos, bad manners, and inappropriate use. However, as long as you follow the basic rules and are considerate of other people, you are always welcome at an *onsen*.

◀ **Notes** ▶ •

chloride 塩化物　　**sore muscle** 筋肉痛

4 Focus: T or F

1) A *Sentō* is a public bath with hot natural water.   T / F

2) A great view from an *onsen* helps blood circulation.   T / F

3) *Onsen* owners like customers with tattoos.   T / F

4) There are some rules for taking a bath at an *onsen*.   T / F

5 Comprehension quiz

Q1. What kind of water is used in an *onsen*?

    a) tap water

    b) natural water

    c) rainwater

    d) seawater

Q2. The physical benefit of an *onsen* is the (　　).

    a) small dressing rooms

    b) view of the *onsen*'s facilities

    c) minerals in the natural water

    d) socializing effects

Q3. *Onsen* are good for your mind because of (　　).

    a) their long history

    b) their inappropriate use

    c) the minerals' effects

    d) the great views

Q4. The social benefit of an *onsen* is that (　　).

    a) it is a place for people to interact

    b) it helps your blood flow

    c) its minerals are good for muscles and skin

    d) it uses water from the public water-system

6 Dialog: Listen to the dialog again and fill in the blanks.

Shunji: Have you submitted your report for biology class?

Mai: Yes. I did it yesterday. Now I need a rest. (1：)?

Shunji: Not yet. But I think I (2：) today. I'm already thinking about how to chill out after I turn it in.

Mai: Why don't we go to an *onsen*?

Shunji: *Onsen*? (3：)?

Mai: It is a public bath, but there's more to *onsen* than that.

Shunji: For example?

Mai: For example, minerals in hot natural water are good for your (4：) and help you recover from tiredness.

Shunji: Nice! I didn't know about that.

Mai: Also, you might get a nice view from an *onsen* bath and have a little chat with other people. Doing that is really good for your (5：).

Shunji: (6：)!

Mai: I'll go online and search for a nice *onsen* near here.

a. Sounds perfect b. Isn't that just a public bath

c. mental refreshment d. How about you

e. muscles and joints f. can finish it

7 Short writing

Do you like *onsen*? Why, or why not?

Unit 13 *How to avoid sleep debt*

 1 Dialog: Listen and answer the following questions.

Q1. Which is considered to be bad manners in public in the US?

a.

b.

c.

Q2. Why does the woman feel so sleepy?

a.

b.

c.

Q3. What might you get if you do not get enough sleep?

a.

b.

c.

2 Words and phrases

1) label	( )	a. 気分の落ち込み
2) heal	( )	b. 脳卒中
3) chronically	( )	c. を分類する
4) debt	( )	d. 慢性的に
5) catch up on ...	( )	e. を癒す
6) stroke	( )	f. 〜の不足を取り戻す
7) depression	( )	g. 負債

3 Reading: How to avoid sleep debt

(39) How many hours do you sleep every night? Six hours? Eight hours? If you don't sleep enough every night, it may cause you a lot of problems. Sleep is a curative* activity — while you sleep, your brain is labeling information and healing your body. Sleeping also heals and repairs your blood vessels and
5 heart.

You can make up missed sleep the next night. If you have to get up early for an appointment on a Friday, and then sleep in on Saturday, you'll mostly recover your missed sleep. However, when you lose sleep chronically, this creates a "sleep debt." That will make it harder to catch up on sleep and
10 increase the probability of signs of lack of sleep. Chronically losing sleep is likely to cause many health problems. It can put you at an increased risk for weight gain, diabetes, a weakened immune system*, heart disease, stroke, high blood pressure, and memory loss. You might also have higher levels of cortisol*, a stress hormone. This can lead to anger, depression, and even
15 suicidal thoughts*.

(40) If you lose sleep chronically, how should you make up for your lost sleep? Here are some ways you can sleep better at night.

· Take a nap of about twenty minutes in the early afternoon.

· Sleep on the weekends, but not more than two hours past the usual
20 time you get up.

· Go to bed a little earlier the next night.

· Stop using electronic devices two hours before bedtime.

◀ Notes ▶ •

curative（誤りを）正す、健康を回復する   **immune system** 免疫システム   **cortisol** コルチゾール
suicidal thoughts 自殺念慮

4 Focus: T or F

1) Lack of sleep can make you unhealthy.   T / F
2) Even when you sleep, your brain works.   T / F
3) "Sleep debt" is a sign of oversleeping.   T / F
4) "Sleep debt" may harm mental health as well as physical health.   T / F

5 Comprehension quiz

Q1. While you sleep, what does your brain do?

    a. cures your body

    b. makes up your body

    c. labels your body parts

    d. catches your body

Q2. When lack of sleep mounts up, what will NOT happen to you?

    a. diabetes

    b. heart disease

    c. depression

    d. weight loss

Q3. When you lose sleep, what might you develop?

    a. high fever

    b. depression

    c. cough

    d. toothache

Q4. What should you do when you have "sleep debt"?

    a. sleep for three hours more on weekends

    b. take a nap for half an hour in the afternoon

    c. avoid using a smartphone a few hours before going to bed

    d. sleep for a fixed time every night

6 Dialog: Listen to the dialog again and fill in the blanks.

Mai: (Yawn)

Sam: (1 :   )

Mai: Excuse me. Yawning in public is bad manners in the US, isn't it?

Sam: Yes, it is. (2 :   )

Mai: I don't have much time to sleep every night. I have only had three or four hours of sleep a night for the last few months.

Sam: Wow! You must be suffering (3 :   )

Mai: Exactly.

Sam: Have you heard of "sleep debt"?

Mai: No. What is it?

Sam: It is when lack of sleep mounts up for a long time, and you're never able to (4 :   ) you lost.

Mai: Ah, Does it have a (5 :   )

Sam: It may cause heart disease or diabetes, or make you easily angry.

Mai: Yes, I've also been angry recently. I think it is because (6 :   )

a. But, why are you so sleepy?　　b. bad effect on your health?

c. I haven't got enough sleep.　　d. catch up on the sleep

e. What a big yawn!　　f. from a lack of sleep!

7 Short writing

What would you say to encourage people to make up for lack of sleep?

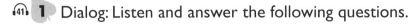
1 Dialog: Listen and answer the following questions.

Q1. Who is suffering from Alzheimer's disease?

a.    b.    c.

Q2. Which part of the body is affected by Alzheimer's disease?

a.    b. 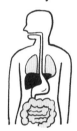   c.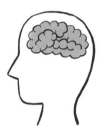

Q3. What is the man worried about?

a.    b.    c.

2 Words and phrases

1) ketone bodies / ketones	( )	a. 症状
2) disorder	( )	b. ブドウ糖
3) progress	( )	c. ケトン体
4) glucose	( )	d. 断食
5) symptom	( )	e. 障害
6) liver	( )	f. 進行する（動詞）、進行（名詞）
7) fasting	( )	g. 肝臓

3 Reading: Alzheimer's disease and the role of ketone bodies

(42)   Alzheimer's is a disease which decreases brain activity due to brain disorders. The disease progresses little by little. People suffering from Alzheimer's start to have trouble in terms of understanding and remembering things. When the disease becomes serious, patients cannot
5 communicate with others or put on their clothes by themselves. In addition, they lose weight and sleep longer. Then they become unable to leave their beds. Since a cure has not yet been found, the progress of the disease cannot be stopped. One of the causes of Alzheimer's is that the brain stops using glucose as an energy source effectively. So, brain cells die and these
10 symptoms appear.

(43)   Some research shows that Alzheimer's patients who took ketone supplements for three months had improved memories. Ketone bodies are called the second energy and are made by the liver. It is known that human beings use them instead of glucose when they are suffering from hunger.
15 The research might suggest that another cause of Alzheimer's is that our bodies are not using ketones.

   Since modern people eat enough every day, there is little chance for our bodies to make and use ketones in our daily life. However, light fasting has recently become popular. Studies have shown that fasting puts our bodies in
20 a state of hunger and that helps our bodies produce ketones. Therefore, studying our eating habits might possibly be a key to preventing Alzheimer's disease.

4 Focus: T or F

1) Once you develop Alzheimer's disease, it cannot be cured.   T / F

2) The internal organ which makes ketone bodies is the brain.   T / F

3) We can produce ketone bodies when we are in a state of hunger.   T / F

4) How to eat is not important to prevent Alzheimer's disease.   T / F

5 Comprehension quiz

Q1. How do the symptoms of Alzheimer's disease progress?

a. slowly

b. quickly

c. not constantly

d. very fast

Q2. What happens to Alzheimer's sufferers' brain cells?

a. They revive.

b. They sleep.

c. They increase.

d. They decrease.

Q3. Why do modern people's livers not make ketone bodies?

a. They have a lot of sugar every day.

b. They have problems with the liver.

c. It is easy to buy ketone supplements at a drug store.

d. They usually do not experience a state of hunger.

Q4. Which of the following might prevent Alzheimer's disease?

a. exercising hard which makes you hungry

b. not eating for a certain period of time

c. eating food that contains a lot of sugar

d. getting up early and going to bed early

Minoru: Naoko, do you know anything about Alzheimer's disease?

Naoko: (1 :   ) Why?

Minoru: My grandfather was diagnosed with Alzheimer's recently.

Naoko: (2 :   ) What kind of disease is it?

Minoru: It's a serious disease, in which the brain stops working normally.

Naoko: (3 :   )

Minoru: Patients have loss of memory, loss of ability to speak clearly and so on.

Naoko: (4 :   ) But that often happens to elderly people, doesn't it?

Minoru: (5 :   ) But Alzheimer's is much more serious.

Naoko: How serious?

Minoru: For example, people with Alzheimer's get lost easily and can't get home when going out alone.

Naoko: I think I've heard about that.

Minoru: He might not recognize me in a few years' time. I really wish there was a cure.

Naoko: (6 :   )

a. What are the symptoms?   b. So do I.

c. Loss of memory?   d. Just the name.

e. I'm sorry to hear that.   f. That's true.

7 Short writing

What are the symptoms of Alzheimer's disease?

Unit 15 Vaccination is one way to prevent influenza

1 Dialog: Listen and answer the following questions.

Q1. What advice is given for preventing colds?

a.

b.

c.

Q2. What is one way to be vaccinated?

a.

b.

c.

Q3. What will Ken do later?

a.

b.

c.

2 Words and phrases

1）vaccination （　　　）
2）influenza / flu （　　　）
3）infection （　　　）
4）virus （　　　）
5）vaccine （　　　）
6）immune system （　　　）
7）side effects （　　　）

a. 免疫システム
b. ワクチン
c. 感染
d. ウイルス
e. 副作用
f. ワクチン接種
g. インフルエンザ

3 Reading: Vaccination is one way to prevent influenza

(45) Influenza is an illness that goes around in Japan every year between December and March. Because the infection spreads rapidly, around 10,000 people die from influenza every year.

There are mainly two ways to become infected. One is through
5 coughing or sneezing. Another way is through direct contact with the virus on surfaces by touching doorknobs or hand straps on trains. In order to prevent infection, you should wear a mask, wash your hands often, and gargle*.

Vaccines are another effective way to prevent the spread of this disease.
10 The basic concept is to inject* a small amount of the virus into a person's body. Their immune system then reacts to the invasion by the virus and creates antibodies*. Later, when exposed to the actual disease, the person's body is prepared to fight it off.

(46) The influenza vaccine can reduce the risk of getting the disease,
15 although the results depend on each individual's condition. In some cases, the vaccine doesn't actually prevent someone from getting the flu, but it can be effective in making the symptoms of the illness milder. Moreover, pregnant women can receive the flu vaccination, and it is effective for their new-born babies as well.

20 Care must also be taken about possible side effects from vaccines, such as headaches, fever, or anaphylactic shock* that may even cause death. Furthermore, travelers may need to get various vaccinations before going to certain foreign countries so they can stay healthy when in different environments.

◀ Notes ▶ ••

gargle うがいする　　**inject** 注射する　　**antibody** 抗体
anaphylactic shock アナフィラキシーショック

58

4 Focus: T or F

1) One hundred thousand people die in Japan from influenza annually.

T / F

2) Influenza can be spread when someone sneezes.   T / F

3) It is safe for pregnant women to get the influenza vaccination.   T / F

4) Travelers don't need to have vaccinations before visiting any foreign countries.

T / F

5 Comprehension quiz

Q1. When do people in Japan often get influenza?

    a. Between August and September

    b. Between October and December

    c. Between December and March

    d. Between April and May

Q2. What is one way that you can become infected with influenza?

    a. By touching door handles

    b. By washing your hands

    c. By transferring trains

    d. By gargling

Q3. What happens sometimes when people get vaccinated for influenza?

    a. It will give the virus to new-born babies.

    b. It will improve a person's condition.

    c. It will make the illness stronger.

    d. It will make the illness milder if the person gets the flu.

Q4. What is one possible side effect of the influenza vaccine?

    a. Electric shock   b. Coughing

    c. Headache   d. Pregnancy

6 Dialog: Listen to the dialog again and fill in the blanks.

Mai: Oh, it's getting colder.

Ken: I don't want to (1：).

Mai: Stay warm and get enough sleep.

Ken: I'm afraid of (2：). It's going around.

Mai: If you get the flu, you will need to stay home for a few days.

Ken: I want to avoid having to do that.

Mai: Did you (3：) this year, Ken?

Ken: I did last year. Do I need (4：) every year?

Mai: Yes. They change the vaccine each year according to the types of flu that are going around.

Ken: Oh really?

Mai: By getting a flu shot you can (5：) of getting the flu.

Ken: OK. I guess I should call my local clinic and make an appointment soon.

Mai: I think that's a good idea, Ken.

Ken: Better safe (6：).

a. catch a cold   b. get vaccinated

c. getting the flu   d. reduce the risk

e. than sorry   f. to get a flu shot

7 Short writing

What is your idea to prevent getting the flu?

明日を生きるこころとからだ

| 検印
省略 | © 2021年1月31日　　第 1 版発行 |

編著者　　　　　　　　　　英米文化学会

赤木大介 / 石川英司 / 佐野潤一郎 /

C.S. Langham / 大東真理 /

田嶋倫雄 / 平田稔 / 松野達 /

発行者　　　　　　　　　　原　雅久
発行所　　　　　　　　株式会社　朝日出版社
101-0065 東京都千代田区西神田3-3-5
電話 (03) 3239-0271
Fax (03) 3239-0479
E-mail text-e@asahipress.com
URL https://text.asahipress.com/english
振替口座　00140-2-46008
組版：明昌堂／製版：錦明印刷

乱丁、落丁本はお取替えいたします。
ISBN978-4-255-15670-5